DOLLS

Also by John Poch

Poems
Ghost Towns of the Enchanted Circle
Two Men Fighting with a Knife

DOLLS

JOHN POCH

John Poch

To Tammy & Will
    Here's to flying high in
Taos!
        Blessings,
            John

ORCHISES

Washington

2009

Copyright © 2009 John Poch

Library of Congress Cataloging-in-Publication Data
Poch, John, 1966-
    Dolls / John Poch.
    p. cm.
    ISBN 978-1-932535-20-4 (alk. Paper)
    I. Title
    PS3616.O28D65 2009
    811'.54—DC22

                                                        2009011396

ACKNOWLEDGMENTS

These journals first published the following poems: *Alabama Literary Review*: "The Missing Child"; *America*: "Simon Peter"; *American Letters and Commentary*: "Not Reading Plato"; *Big Tex[t]*: "The Windmill"; *Blackbird*: "John's Christ"; *Callaloo*: "Gerald Stern, 1992"; *Colorado Review*: "Valle Vidal"; *Communiqué*: "Zaccheus"; *Five Points*: "Ocean"; *Lake Effect*: "5 AM"; *Meridian*: "Forgiveness"; *New Letters*: "The Blue Angels"; *The New Republic*: "The First Star"; *Paris Review*: "February Flu," "Well into Winter; *Passages North*: "Tiger Woods"; *Phoebe*: "Majorette"; *Rivendell*: "Jorie Graham"; *Sewanee Theological Review*: "Seven's Meditation"; *Think Journal*: "Tuesday"; *Unpleasant Event Schedule*: "The Taos Carpenter."

www.thefishouse.org and www.poetrynet.org first published "The Tongue" and "Dolls," respectively. Other poems appeared in a limited edition letterpress book, *Ghost Towns of the Enchanted Circle* (Flying Horse Press, 2007).

"Dear Reader" was first published as "My Best Reader" in a special edition of *STYLE*, essays and poems compiled as a festschrift for the linguist and poet, Háj Ross.

The poems in this book were written with the generous help of The Thornton Writer-in-Residence Fellowship at Lynchburg College and a residency at Headlands Center for the Arts, a Howard Nemerov Fellowship from the 2004 Sewanee Writers Conference, a Dorothy Sargent Rosenberg Award, and a faculty development leave from Texas Tech University.

ORCHISES PRESS
P. O. BOX 320533
ALEXANDRIA, VIRGINIA 22320-4533

G6E4C2A

CONTENTS

for Eavan and Bronwyn

[After the departure of the general,] a child's doll was found in the room, which the younger officers tossed from one to the other, and called the "Silent Witness."

—COLONEL HORACE PORTER of General Ulysses Grant's staff

Appomattox, VA, 1865

When we are alone with them, we are not quite alone.

—JOHN NOBLE

Among my marionettes I find
The enthusiasm is intense!

—T.S. ELIOT

DEAR READER

Denominator,
help me upkeep.
Dying irises, for instance.
Elide the failing finery,
make the failure finer,
cut for the future.
Make a meal of bone
and turn it in.

The less you are...
but do not become nothing.
Rise, kiss me on the mouth
with your small mouth.
Equal me into a line,
a page seen from the side.
Treat me like a treaty signed,
the ink kiss spilled
down both our throats.
Together we will decide
the four saddest words in English history,
whether day or night is praiseworthy,
the folding of the grief industry.
Alter at this altar.

DOLLS

But this being-less-than-a-thing, in its utter irremediability,
is the secret of its superiority.
—RILKE, "Some Reflections on Dolls"

Our local strip club, Baby Dolls, is under
special scrutiny. The owner blundered,
failed to report a former felony.
He'll dress his dolls or face the penalty
of closure. *Clothing or Closed*—the headline raves.
And now appeals are in the works to save
the local gentlemen "their harmless fun."
They love their spices: Ginger, Cinnamon,
and the twins, Brandi and Candi (both with i's),
who intimate a titillating surprise
as to who they really are. But no one's claiming
these strippers toy with the metaphysics of naming,
identity, or grammar.
                   My daughter, one,
blue eyes, gold curls, and skin of porcelain
makes women gasp. They call her doll. They fuss.
One: *Where did you get her, Cherubs-R-Us?*
At home she is her own cruise ship, crawling
a vast expanse of living room while hauling
a doll at her side—a lifeboat dangling, it seems,
by appointment to her majesty, the Queen.
The other dolls left in her wake are like

a flotsam of suicidal beauties who fake
an elegant distress and subtly yearn
a ship with lifeline floats will soon return.
We love how she pretends to care: to hold,
to put to bed, to hug and kiss, or scold
the one whose only fault is being plastic.

To love our families, our friends, we practice
with dolls or animals. We build them houses,
and give them names and pair them up with spouses.
To make us feel that someone has it tougher,
we make the doll, in fifteen minutes, suffer
the hurt or fame it takes a lifetime to
achieve, the fate a real-life G.I. Joe
could not survive. Ken never thinks to flee
a Wheelchair Barbie's disability.
Are they for girls, and will our boys become
effeminate, lose all command, go mum?
The voodoo doll is funny till it looks
like us and someone stabs the hands or cooks
the brains so we rely, like the greenest Muppet,
on tired metaphors and a rhyming couplet.
However, Russian dolls are most like the poet
inside the empty poet, and so on, inchoate
like me inside a Wilbur in a Yeats
in a Browning in a Poe inside a Keats.
These wind up on a shelf in the family room,
are rarely touched, but then there's Harold Bloom.

We know that Rilke's mother yearned so much for
a girl, she made him wear, till he was four,
a dress. She foisted on her little doll
(middle name, Maria) a little doll,
an image of himself, herself. And thus,
Rilke learned, the hard way, dolls answer us,
like God and Destiny, with silence, a soul,
a doll-soul, quiet as a bullet hole.
Charles Baudelaire thought children ache to see
so passionately the soul within a toy,
they dash it on walls, throw it to the ground
until it spills its stuffing and nothing, profound,
expands the emptiness of that playroom.
And thus begins our melancholy, gloom.

Does God play house with us—or even stranger,
do we make God a doll, complete with manger?
Did Jesus have a doll, a nativity set,
or Joseph carve him a wooden chariot
and pugilists who punch each other over
who gets to be Ben Hur, who gets to chauffeur.

We dress, undress, and leave our dolls in poses.
We flee the graven image and climb like Moses
having put away our childish things (St. Paul),
to take the hand of God. Or a different doll:
a pet, a friend, a mirror, beau, or lover.
We know ourselves by virtue of another.

My little girl, that doll I deify,
dress up, wind up, screw up, and let her fly,
she'd rather hug her man, Pinocchio,
than me. Already, I have to let her go.
I'm proud as Punch she looks and acts somewhat
like me: her sunken Russian cheeks, her strut.
But life's provisional as furniture.
I should know better than to worship her.
For God, who took from Job and then required
from Abraham by his own hand (but spared)
his son, demands that I relinquish all
my loves, for He is great and I am small.

While we have art to save us from the Truth,
we know the fountain of eternal youth
runs dry, and though its marble nudes are massive
gods, they corrode, are ultimately passive:
the sexy figure, Henri Moore's weird bronzes,
on film, James Bond, played this time by Pierce Brosnan,
with a bevy of dolls, yet poor Miss Moneypenny...

At Baby Dolls, some wise guy thinks he's funny:
A dollar for the doll, he slips his five
beneath her garter. She makes it come alive,
it disappears, he looks her up and down
upon her pedestal. A mere pronoun,
she leans against the pole as if to suffer
a different kind of passion, as if no lover,

no proper gentleman will ever touch her.
She strolls the strobe-lit stage where all must judge her.
He's loud, has drunk too much: *Me Tarzan, you Jane.*
He bares his chest; she's not allowed. In vain,
she looks away to the mirror across the room,
and briefly wonders who she fools or whom.

THE TONGUE

The scriptures call it wicked, hypocrite,
the bridle turning the horse to war,
the rudder the ship to rocks,
cursing as it will before the wreck,
after the interception, during the bus ride home
where we tried the various fricatives
in the rebellion of our youth.

While one child's first word is *this,*
and another tries to capture
her mother's single words with her fist,
and yet another asks at bedtime,
Daddy, how much is night?
—my toddler daughter only sticks out
her tongue at the word *tongue,*
her small, moist strawberry of a tongue
she seems to eat when I reach for it
with forefinger and thumb.
She is an alien to me sometimes.
When she head-thuds the table edge,
her tongue becomes an alien in an alien
rearing its ugly tongue-of-a-head.

Paul Klee said he wanted all his life
to paint like a child. He did, eventually,
which is one reason we should have

Surrealist action figures. A man
across the hall has X-Files dolls
of Scully and Mulder on his desk.
I remember how, for seven years,
we begged the TV, *Please, Chris
Carter, let them kiss, just once.*
Our tongues wagged at the monstrous
interruptions: The Cigarette-Smoking Man,
The Well-Manicured Man, all conspiracies
against their love we knew was more
than friendship or fuzzy spaceship worship.
Their secret passion was sealed
like an X-file we knew existed,
forbidden, in a folder almost hidden
like a mouth and its tongue
that couldn't state the facts
but could taste the story.
Let me tell you a story:

In another life my daughter will speak
with her tongue, be a wife,
say *My name is Eavan, I do,
I do not like them with a fox,*
will kiss a boy on the mouth,
will fall, will fill a boy's eyes
with her eyes, her mother's French eyes,
sleepy, almost always moving toward this kiss.

In another life, judging by their names,
(listen to their names)
Fox Mulder and Dana Scully
could have been rodeo lovers—
one calf-roper, the other, barrel racer.
But here they were each week, one believer,
one doubter, both traveling toward the same
afflicted podunk town in some brown sedan.
So often, they looked at each other
as purely as the U.S. looks at Canada.
Then they looked away.

Out of the mouth proceed
both cursing and blessing,
both lie and utter truth,
and one late fall, in the thick of sweeps,
another episode at the edge
of the millennium, near the end
of seven seasons, we wanted nothing more
than the kiss between the two.
I wanted a French kiss.

for Austin Hummell

Naming a Child

A dozen scaled quail weave their worried patter
through the sage brush to our back porch.
I cluck and the lookout mother
on the bush perks up. Chicks scatter.
An orange wasp mauls passionately the spearmint flowers.
An old story, the birds and bees come to summer.

Waking just an hour ago,
I watched you shift within
your mother's belly in the morning sun
like someone kneading dough
from inside out, awkwardly comic
but sacramentally sure in your work,
your play. On the stage of the wet desert dust,
this humble mud, did the blood-bright sun wake you
and, with last night's brief rain, make you
something new like an adobe church
whose rounded buttresses breathe, shine,
and shadow in the first long light?

How can I care for ghost towns and mining
when the clouds look like fat horses
leaping from the mountains?
I know the hands of old men trembled
when whole gold nugget buddhas

like tiny babies tumbled
from the quartz veins in these mountains,
but the blonde tufts of those quail
and the hunger of the wasp shine now.
Little actor, play within a play,
body at the center of a body,
nearly mythic beloved of mine
and heaven and the birds between,
I am your audience applauding.
My prayer: turn toward the light the same
as you will turn toward your name.

WHEN YOU HEAR YOUR NAME

Ask a jewel how the atoms
in you were born in stars.
God-like in love,
you make-up your cupcake poem,
you poet, you bracelet
about a living room.
Your scarf tumbles humbly
like a winded sycophant,
happiest at rest on your breast
below a burning cigarette.

But remember, at the ash end,
if you're lucky, all that will be left:
your name stamped on a leaden drainpipe.
If you're luckier: Zinedene Zidane.

JOHN POCH

A smaller Jackson Pollock, my polar blues
in cursive curse and scratch. A wasted fire
to write myself lies scribbled, smolders. Moods
instead of house-high flames' emotion mire
a vision. Ink, they lie. I thought my trifle
of a title clever as a bell. No tongue,
for days I pooled, cooled, and dried, lay stifled.
The sticks of spite, coyote bones I slung
at others, stir my wreckage, violin me.
A ghost town's last home in my chair—my lap
foundation and the rest extinguished chimney—
I hover above my sonnet, my handicap
apparent, arson on the brain, and practice
denying my death, patient as practice practice.

JORIE GRAHAM

No one likes to lie or be lied to.
—JORIE GRAHAM

Once, I pressed my ear
against a doorframe in Iowa.
Picture a lover fresh from his beloved
trying hard to become a doorframe
through which that beloved will walk
and even sleepwalk. Listen.
Ants were eating the house,
and you could hear their fun.
The workers were so drunk with crunching
they would stagger out
from the baseboard like total tourists.
And I, a skyscraper.
The queen lay safe a hundred yards away,
which seemed a mile, while poem
after poem dropped from her body.
These were carried away
before she could mature them.
I am not obsessed with the queen.
I am not obsessed with the queen.
I am not obsessed with the queen.
She made me write this a hundred times
on the board after class one year.
The workers made fun and crunched.

The queen said, This boy is a liar;
now laugh at him. I stood
accused of imitating a doorframe,
of writing a sonnet.
I wish this were a sonnet.
I wish everything were one.
I stood there with my ear
like a flag on a pole
contemplating hospitality or revenge.
I chose nectar—that which overcomes death—
and I poured it on.

GERALD STERN, 1992

All the great poets lived in Pennsylvania,
he told me. Since he knew I was from Erie,
PA, it wasn't exactly egomania.
He was from Pittsburgh, he said, and *Call me Gerry.*

He sort of meant it: Merwin, Gilbert, Stevens.
And Pound at college with guess who? H.D.!
But then he noted, *Ginsberg might have forgiven
Pound for the Jews, but he didn't forgive him for me.*

He claimed that "Dover Beach" was boring, at most.
When I dissented, he took to calling me "The Preacher."
And he told me he was studying the Holy Ghost.
I talked to the janitor about my teacher.

Gerry? he said. *The guy who wails like a baby
down the street blessing all the mailboxes?* Maybe.

TIGER WOODS

*He has not thrust down his youth untried
into a place where splendors are hidden.*
—PINDAR, *Isthmia VIII*

Twelve yards past Daly on the drives, he makes
the par-five green in two despite the woods.
When he went pro he'd just turned twenty-one,
an instant millionaire: both down to earth
and off the scale—from birdies made per round
to eagle frequency. The news: "It was,"
his mother Tida boasted, "like he was
the pope!" at Disney World that year. (He makes,
without a white golf cart, his holy rounds.)
Followers out of fairways, out of the woods,
now congregate so closely they hear the earth
swept by his swing—but they cannot see. For one,
the crowds are tripled now. And two, no one
can catch this Nike swoosh before it *was*,
before we sense the shudder of the earth.

A Neiman blur, he is the art he makes.
The galleries hang on his tee shot three woods
outdriving drivers nearly every round.
He widens the world of sports. He makes it round
and rests and calls it good. Come, hole-in-one.
Never caught off guard with *coulds* or *woulds*

before the human press, he is, and was
always, a student of the game, making
the grades. We never knew the greens of earth
could be so colorful. Who on earth
could bring an age of racial strife around
to these fair ways, afternoons of peace-making?
The kid who's "fundamentally sound," says one
Jack Nicklaus, The Golden Bear. Tiger was
chipping "before he could walk," insists Earl Woods.

I think there are most tigers in the wood
—from Wilbur's "Ceremony," now unearths
a different rite: our Sunday news. What was
a birdie turns to eagle. Stick around.
What's nestled in the toughest rough is one
more opportunity to prove what makes
a man a hero here on earth. The woods
applaud another round, cry out, *He was*
made for a make of jacket. The green one.

SIMON PETER

I.

Contagious as a yawn, denial poured
over me like a fall fog. I was a pearl
all swallowed by its oyster flesh, caving
and covering hurt, feigning boring and bored.
A robed commotion passed us, armed and raving.
I turned and turned away and turned. A swirl

of wind pulled back my hood, a fire took hold
and brightened my face, and those around me whispered:
You're one of them, aren't you? You smell like fish.
And wine, someone else joked. That's brutal. That's cold,
I said, and then they knew me by my speech.
They let me stay and we told jokes like fisher-

men and houseboys. We gossiped till the cock crowed,
his head a small volcano raised to mock stone.

II.

Who could believe a woman's word, perfumed
in death? I did. I ran and was outrun
before I reached the empty tomb. I stepped
inside an empty shining shell of a room.
No pearl. I walked back home alone and wept
again. At dinner, his face shone like the sun.

I stole into the night. I was a sailor
and my father's nets were calling. It was high tide,
I brought the others. Nothing, the emptiness
of business, the hypnotic waves of failure.
But a voice from shore, a familiar fire, and the nets
were full. I wouldn't be outswum, denied

this time. The fire before me, the netted fish
behind. I'm carried where I will not wish.

ZACCHEUS

The news of Bartamaeus' sight
precedes you, Lord, who look toward
another miracle. I'm slight,
caught hanging in a sycamore

along your route through Jericho.
These leprous limbs almost disguise
how like a little child I go
these foolish lengths to flee the lies

I sell my brothers for a profit.
I know the scriptures—how Naaman tried
to buy his healing from the prophet,
complained about the Jordan tide,

its filthy silt. And yet he swam
and rose up with a newborn skin.
Out of the dusty human din
below the sycamore, my name.

The silence ripens; then, this tree
must seem alive to all who see
its sway and hear the tree bark splinter.
I'm coming down to wash for dinner.

ICARUS, REJECTED

His canceled self-addressed stamped envelope
looked like a little pillow, all feathers and down!
All feathers and down, R.I.P., you dope.

the foul note replied. There went his hope.
But there was more. *Cloud to town. Dream to noun.*
His canceled self addressed stamped envelope

with his poetry manuscript: *A tired trope.*
Your melted ice cream sundae pile of brown.
All feathers and down, R.I.P., you dope.

Stay off the drugs. None of your beeswax. Nope.
and more: *A dead baby in a baptism gown.*
His canceled self addressed stamped envelope

held *a hard pill to swallow. A pillow?* How could he cope
with: *Flown. On your own. A bandage for your crown?*
All feathers and down, R.I.P., you dope.

Mother's smile to smothered frown. No Pope,
the Editor added, *drown in drool, you clown,*
you canceled self addressed stamped envelope,
all feathers and down, R.I.P., you dope.

THE ROMANTIC

He was tired of poems other poets wrote.
He broke all the rules, and the rules he made up broke.

He was down with the language of men, of Bloods and Crips,
and he wrote with the feeling of rejection slips.

The quill of his pen was plucked from a royal bird,
but his left-hand chicken scratch made the script absurd.

His blood was ink and not a private act.
He spilled it like a hemophiliac.

He thought the books he burned rather than wrote
were smoke signals, rather than signals of smoke.

He thought his lover watched from the distant hills.
She was sleeping off her love of sleeping pills.

His wine was almost extra virgin nectar,
but she was ruined. The cork was loose and wrecked her.

He saw God as a distant Oversoul,
and God declared, *For Christmas he'll get coal.*

His cape was made of freshest armadillo.
At night it doubled as his hard-earned pillow.

He dreamed on the banks, and banked on his dreams and smoke.
When the river crested, broke, he never woke.

John's Christ

The auctioneer commits his little gaffe
as helpers lift the latch-hook tapestry
of Leonardo's Christian masterpiece:
The Large Supper. The waiting bidders laugh.

And though the latest spiritual fad has raptured
a populace of New Age novel-lovers,
DaVinci's purpose is better left to others.
But here at our local auction I am captured,

wanting to lean, like John, away from the master,
get some perspective on His hands, the gist
of one opening, one closing, not a fist,
His arms apart, beholding, Jesus' gesture

over his empty plate and the rag-tag cast
preparing for the word, *large,* or *last.*

THE TAOS CARPENTER

Like almost any carpenter, he curses God
when he hits his hand with a hammer.
A man so long working with trees,
he likes his shade, the breeze, but more,
the stillness. Leaning his back against the cottonwood,
he calls his girlfriend, saying, Punkin, saying,
Baby-love. He lets his dog out of the truck,
pouring him another bowl of water.
He puts his dog back in the truck.
He misses the days of hand-planing
an entire cabin's-worth of floor boards,
though he never owned a plane.
He lets his dog out of the truck.
The board feet in a nearby ponderosa pine
are intuition to him, and groove means many things.

He can be humble.
On his break, he writes a two-line poem
for his book of two-line poems:

God has nails in his hand.
And there goes a man with the hammer.

SUPERMAN

In our real-life adaptation of the movie,
the heroine who needs a helping hand,
my distraught daughter, lifts him, broken, to me.
What role do I play on this stage? The man

behind the curtain, best boy, grip, or gaffer?
Who's saving whom from what? What's Kryptonite?
The weight of sin in an action figure laugher?
What can I do for you, a type of the Christ,

for a heart surprisingly like ours: fun,
lonely, tempted by power and flattery,
susceptible to fate, love, and done.
Game over.
        I replace your battery.

Doll, who am I above your resurrection:
a bird, a plane, your image, The Great Affection?

THE CROSS

You can make one with your fingers,
your hands, your whole body.
A common tattoo.
A corkscrew gone through itself,
away from the wine and into the hand.
The simplest arm of a broken snowflake.
Pure outdoor torture furniture.
A Roman invention, but more important—a human invention.
Sexy on a rock star's throat.
Does it make you mad? angry? cross?
Don't cross me.
Don't cross your eyes. They'll stay that way.
Cross yourself. Stay that way.
Cross your heart? Hope to die?
A rose staked up, thorns and blooming all over. All over.
A wet but drying double-crested cormorant hangs across the air.
Mortal support.
The new math.
For instance, time's crossroads times zero equals infinity.
A plus.
Death's Leer jet, seen from below.
A God's-eye view of a rush-hour intersection, crawling.
An old phone pole, calling.
Two high beams coming at you, blinding you.
The X of a kiss, turned a little tighter.

The X of murder turned a little tighter.

The X of buried treasure, found, turned a little tighter.

A lower case t, sans serif, sans seraphim.

The word torture has two t's.

This poem has exactly one hundred t's, all crossed.

Do you wish to cross-examine?

To a tee. To a tree.

Excruciatingly double crossed.

A million potential splinters.

The scarecrow that works forever.

Someone waits on a hill in silhouette.

SEVEN'S MEDITATION

O God of Passion's Earthquake, the six o'clock report
is over. Surprising weather, decisions of the court,
our Neighbor's public horror shared equal time with sport.

For certain, the news got worse at the point of sin's long arrow.
We heard what sounded like the twittering of a sparrow,
but it had been a prophet sweating blood and marrow,

refusing a joke of a drink above the acid laughter.
The finished sun was heavy, slumping down the rafters.
At seven, we thought the news was over, jeopardy after.

But someone had to get a tomb and hold a wake
and keep the body from the jackals for the sake
of Peter, James, and John all fallen in the quake.

Perverse, the wooden anchor which held the air to earth,
plowing a trench in heaven, gripping, hard, and death
came down in bloody chains, a body out of breath.

Since no one fathoms what transpires within a tomb,
nor what happens when unanchored from the womb
and spirited into a clement, light-filled room,

to keep the earth from drifting off the face of heaven,
and vice versa, I dwell on this good news seven
times seven times seven times seven times seven times seven times seven.

FORGIVENESS

Because justice must recede
like a page number
and because the dictionary of under
is a tedious read, more simply
consider the ground
as those who pour concrete
think of how it rained or will.

Consequently, consider the sky,
and pray like a murderer has died.
When a person dies,
it's not a page ripped out
of a book. It's a chapter
in another language
nearly written.

When toasting your rival,
let the glass fall
with your hand, but hold
the glass.
Give up *because.*

If we must bury the hatchet,
then you be the priest.

THE BLUE ANGELS

Did God make them?
They blanket, carpet, cover us
at the air show. Decorators
with a vengeance. So this is why
the sky is blue. There is sick sadness
in every departure. Far away,
they could be geese in winter travel.
Closer, they are bruisers thundering
tunes of bruises, blooming, almost
shattering every second. Batterers,
they go screaming away from a scream.

A soul under every heavy-lidded,
heavenward eye. Nearly human,
they weep, but they weep fast fire.
The angels come at each other
like two fingers with the eyes closed.
They make passes at each other,
nearly erotic, perpetually young.
They miss, of course. In robes of smoke,
one watches over each shoulder.
The voice of one says *peace*, the other
war. They are a pain in the neck.
Hard to believe they don't kill each other.
No. Hard to believe they don't kill us.
We make them.

THE WINDMILL

Above the world's immensest aquifer,
I stand abandoned like an idiot
struck by the wind, an arrested officer.

Sentence me, Dante, to fruitful tedium.
If I were purged of passive voice, I'd move
myself to irrigation's idiom.

Ravens built a barbed-wire nest above
my steel-backed babbitted bearings. A marbling
runs down my neck from their cloacal uncouth.

The tongues of Ogallala's babbling
should be my glossolalia, my liquid mirth
of humming to drown the rusted warbling

of the black brood stabbing the sky for all they're worth—
a hunger for blood and dust. And though I rest,
a mere old battered scaffold here on Earth,

Texas, due east of Farwell, a wind-gust west
of Plainview's woes, like Bartimaeus, blind,
naked, leaning toward the sun, I confess

conversion thirst in history's gears, the kind
that hold the earth to sky and roar to growl.
Imagine the metal teeth of wind and wind

and not precisely knowing the sound of the vowel
content with being blown, until, turning
forward, clockwise with a holy howl:

a blade, then space, a blade, then space, churning
and drawing water from the earth, not oil,
till longhorn drift like snow above the burning

miles of almost useless iron soil.
I'm not James Dean's dirty derrick in Giant,
but a windmill, grinding arid air, loyal

to the continent. Utterly un-Hawaiian,
amazed at rain and poet-lonely, I am
this stationary, long-necked, high plains lion.

MAJORETTE

The peacocks at the monastery
serve two purposes. The monks pray,
tossing hunks of bread
to the gnarled heads,
This is my pride, don't tell,
take and eat. The peacocks swell.

My gnarled brain escapes me.
Instead, I am a majorette finished
acting like she breathes just fine.
And yet...sequin, sequin, sequin,

while someone, somewhere, is taking
a fugue exam
to end all fugue exams.

VALLE VIDAL

Like a cutthroat
in a meadow stream,
I look upstream, through a disturbance.
And I see you,
looking up through a disturbance,
a cutthroat.

The water is clear as a window with sheets
of rainwater running over it,
and I stand here as one who waits
for someone I need to appear.

Some say the orange gash below your gills
is a repository of a sixth sense.
If you could thirst, this is how you thirst.
Your patience amazes, as you wait
for the stonefly nymph to rise, molt, lift,
and then you fly as if to teach the stonefly
flight. Again, you wait below a boulder
watching the river pass as I wait
below a mountain watching the stream pass.
Your green algae drifts in the current.
My willows stream above the stream
with the wind of a coming storm.
God is watching.

How could I be a fisher of men
had I never stood in moving water
with an invisible line between my hands
and a multitude of choosing and mending,
if I had not turned over the most unremarkable
of rocks and apprenticed to an insect,
if I had not witnessed the orange prisms of dew
dropping from the tips of spearmint leaves
touched by the small breeze cleansing this place?

MUSEUMS

You can't live there.
—JOHN ASHBERY

Neither do they give us bread or haircuts,
and yet they've seen fit to transplant
this house corner to this museum corner,
as it was with fresco wall and mosaic floor,
and some hand-size tiles vase-patterned
in blue, the feminine curves full
and repeated every fourth tile,
painted by a hand that knew,
perhaps that loved or loved to watch
and touch, a pregnant woman and fruit.
On a shelf we see the human bones,
the coins, the bone nails, the bone needles,
a fishing net needle, a fishing net weight,
a loom weight, and some ceramic rooftop
complete with a stuffed sparrow perched.
The mosaic: a child riding a gold wolf.
Who takes the time to stuff a sparrow?
We live between the wolf and the sparrow.

MUSEUM PIECE

The night comes early
with its Rothko Chapel purple.
Just-post-winter solstice,
and little crystals start to fern and surface
in the museum window corners.
A thin translucent flint scraper
lies detached from its history, safer
under glass, beside a little card.

Outside, December kestrels have come—
little fiercenesses clenched like barbs
on a long wire humming in the plain wind.
Except to the mouse surprised and pinned,
the face stains are funny feathers
if you see them.

Halfway to death, I need a museum
with an unearthly, unearthed,
brittle eagle bone flute.
I feel a different winter weather
when I want this rarest note—
to breathe into a hollow below myself.
My shirt smells like my father.

The First Star

—Hamilton, NY

There are no paperwhites on the meadow edge
this time of year; only snow that shimmers
like paperwhite petals in the farewell window
of March's postponed clemency, dune-blown
with skirt-pretty ripples. Like someone cared.
Why come out here and think of paperwhites
bent toward a window with their clustered cups
of six-tricks listening when half a dozen deer
stand prey-still on the valley's facing hill?
The sound of my own voice substitutes
for the voice of God. *Here I am.* And, of course,
the sudden windscatter on snow like sand.
A few maples clacking. The day dies,
and an invisible coydog pack descends
on the fawn of my optimism. The first star
hovers out of nowhere. For courage's sake,
I think it real as a blown flag shadow.
But it could be the spark in air at the end
of a whip on the back of a nightmare.

THE MISSING CHILD

Like token feathers plucked from a broken bird,
the parents are separated from their daughter.
The dresses on their hangars don't say a word,
and slumping like a dirty shirt, the father
wears unaware his stains. What was labor
and what was a given? Breathing was a given.
The mother dreams she is her own neighbor
who has a living daughter. The father is driven
livid by men in suits and women in jewels.
The parents, when they put on their masks and walk
away from each other as those who pace in duels,
keep walking with their faith turned dumbest luck
and accordions for lungs. Her birthday chair
is light and heavy, like cake flour. Or air.

WELL INTO WINTER

The moon goes down like a coin. Spent,
even memory is becoming a memory.

Any tree would seem to grieve,
what with the hawk lonelinessing
on her desiccated perch,
her feathers the opposite of snow.

The day has never been so much the night
and vice versa. And the afternoon
never so much the afternoon.
Meanwhile, meanwhile.

Years ago, a child put a coin
in the crook of this tree.
Now, the sun is drawn up
like a pail from a well.
The pail is poured out and snow.

TUESDAY

Two pages stuck together,
the poet's weather,
less act, less scene,
between the moon and sea,
the brief wave that might have been
on the ordinary beach,
the watermark of the week
has come unbeckoned
and as quickly goes. Teach
us your verse, brief
poem, sandpiper's beak
of days. The citizen reckoned,
among men of arms a hand,
second.

FEBRUARY FLU

Month of the least death poetry,
I pity you: a bone of a day
once every four years tossed your way.
You bury it.

A fever coming on, a swoon
and syrup filling up a spoon.
There's time for only one full moon.
You carry it.

The heart of you is candy hearts,
symmetrical, sans blood. Cruel arts,
Pandora's chocolate box with chart:
you ferry it,

seven by four, across the air
in snowshoes, open it to share
the blizzard of love's polar bear.
I marry it.

A Skeleton Get Well

We stick around as long as possible.
Even the washed up oil-spill pelican.
You know it's not just flesh that feels the pull

to live a little longer. Float as if full
of air when sick to death and salad-thin.
We stick around as long as possible,

so why not you despite the void and null
of eating only Saltines and gelatin.
You know? It's not just flesh that feels the pull,

that elasticity of a baby's skull.
Hang on like closet-knocking skeletons
and stick around as long as possible.

Who cares that summer doesn't follow fall?
No matter what size font I spell it in,
you know, it's not just flesh that feels the pull.

I give to you this skinny key: Get well.
From afar, I pray this ball joints bulletin:
Stick around. As long as possible.
You know it's not just flesh that feels the pull.

5 AM

People want four things. The first three
are easy: to love, to know, to be.
The fourth is for the rooster atop
the bush outside my window to stop
its lonely crowing. For sleep's sake,
even the cat thinks what will it take
to figure his pretty hen is dead.
Shredded feathers and fluff were spread
across the yard outside the back door
like a shuttlecock factory floor.
From darkness, he calls her nonetheless,
till the stars have faded in the west.
Some morning soon I might take him
by the old comb and beak and shake him,
look him in the eye and say, She won't
be back, not now, not noon, so don't,
just don't. But then, I allow the blame
of betrayal is better than the shame
of silence. I get up, crow along,
singing some forlorn morning song
while poaching eggs. Silence comes
with eating. I throw the few toast crumbs
of what's left over into the back yard
along with last night's corn and Swiss chard,
and who comes barreling over to look

but this dumb bird who daily crooks
his neck to crow when he sees the sun
like a distant yolk not quite a son,
not quite a god, when he lifts his praise
to mystery and emptiness.

NOT READING PLATO

Plato in hand as I lean back into pillows.
The crumple of the hood from the car wreck
in my dream last night, it now occurs to me,
was not my fault because I was backing up.
Strange to recuperate a dream while,
in the kitchen, an iron skillet seasons.
No oven light—I have to imagine
the pan. It must look like a grackle,
great-tailed handle flung away from the cave
of itself, haughty in the shade, one eye turned
to tree, one to the hope of more than cinders.
If I lift the idea of the grackle-pan
suddenly in sunlight, I picture the funny papers
on fire, a color caving, a surface turning.
A flash past the real window of the room suggests
a real grackle just flew past. Backing up to
backing into the car wreck, judging from the hood,
someone backed into me. Reader, back me up,
come back with me, your grackle in shadow.
Call a wrecker, take my word, your backhoe-size
black hole of a body's memory. Remember me,
or the image of me dropping the book and quitting the room,
pulling the tail of the pan from the cave of the oven
and holding something almost flaming, waving heat,
something worth preserving, up to the light.

OCEAN

Lagos, Portugal

When the wind comes off the ocean, a patina
of haze warms the hillside facing the marina.
White buildings step up into a sort of slum,
a bulwarks, then tourist condominiums
outside the old town walls, the smell of nets
drying in the January dusk.
Time is forgotten in the rush of business,
but now it is a street light in the distance
coming on, perfecting our vacation,
a pretend-star in some constellation
of the earth's twilight. This morning, in front of us,
an old woman crossed the marina full of sailboats.
The handle on one of her grocery bags
full of eels broke. The largest eel burst out,
writhed and heaved its painful smile from side
to side suddenly remembering water.
She stomped its head with her black boot.
Her dress was black, and women still wear black
in Portugal if their husbands die or go afar.
Later at the market we saw her leaning
on a churro cart, drinking medronho,
lost in some private vision we'll never know.
She didn't recognize us, had sold her eels
apparently. Is the Portuguese chimney

she lives below unique as the others here?
The chimneys are little covered Parthenons
or Pantheons, or chicken crates on end
or modest chapels, steeples, or birdcages
or ghosts of or memorials for birdcages,
granite or cement or ceramic, mostly white.

The boys in the vacant lot above the hillside
falling down to the placid ocean toward
the south are building bike ramps from mounds
of red dirt, bricks, and warped and broken boards
left over from the new construction site.
It seems they shush each other as they play.
And just beyond, on a typical seaside stretch
of stone-strewn hills, two dozen ragtag cows
graze above the sea. Their two front legs
are tied with short gray ropes to keep them close,
to keep them from running. They don't mind.
In a year, another awkward condo and lawns
and palm trees from Morocco's north will blind
whoever sits here with balconies, windows,
perhaps a reflection of the setting sun.
Gone, the cows, this ocean view, the tuna boats
passing, and a boat with a single fisherman
a couple hundred meters out so minute
I barely see him. He's letting out a net
without end. He represents Time.
Who is to blame for the dread in the sublime

sad net pulled up, or the black boot crushing a smile,
or diesel staining the buildings at their crowns,
muting the white in the feathers of the storks?
My little girl comes out to the patio
with her talking doll to interrupt the regret
I force onto the white scene, the pleasant shadows,
the well-weathered Portuguese, old, young, and cows.
Each morning before sunrise she points to town
and the lights saying something like *Lagos* and then
to our ephemeral ocean saying, *ocean.*

for Douglas Inglis

A SECOND CHILD

The whitewashed interior of this seaside church
whose vaults are typical (the Gothic arches
sculpted into ropes) remains otherwise plain
with dark pews and, at the rear, a granite font.
Yet, in a corner, some playful mason carved a hand
holding the rope. I hold your hand like a rope
of mystery with levity as we tour
the church while someone else's tour guide drones
about Our Lady worshipped here, her child.

The recent mural of the Crucified
behind the altar makes a kitschy contrast
with the architecture's unpretentious past,
and one wonders why the latest microphones
among so much echoing stucco and stone.
No whispered secret could be kept here.
The historical site of the first great European
slave market lies just across the plaza,
graffitied, vacant, and no one stops for long.
Great stories become small. The ancient truth—
against the sand and jetties, the constant crash.

You and I, and a toddler orbiting,
amid great circumstance, the lasting facts
of another people's history, done

with the church, we walk into the whiter day
of seagulls and sun, the clatter of nesting storks,
past café patios through streets and sidewalks
of countless inlaid stones to a plaza where someone
a hundred years ago with sea-glass-green
ceramic tile saw fit to cover one wall
of an entire building. We have time to drink
a coffee, try some almond and fig croissant,
and sit on a bench near the simple fountain
in the sun. Close your eyes and imagine pink
or the blue of Mary's dress as long as you want.